Contents

Cover Design • Temple of Design
Cover Photo • Stockbyte

Order No. 1140a
ISBN No. 1-857200446

Exclusive Distributors:
Walton Manufacturing Co. Ltd.
Unit 6A, Rosemount Park Drive, Rosemount Business Park,
Ballycoolin Road, Blanchardstown, Dublin 15, Ireland

Walton Music Inc.
P.O. Box 874, New York, NY 10009, U.S.A.

Printed in Ireland by ColourBooks Ltd.

3 5 7 9 0 8 6 4 2

I Know Where I'm Going

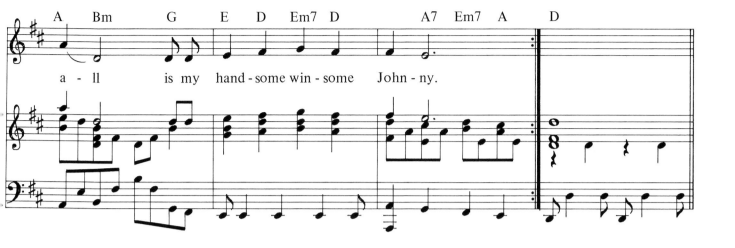

a - ll is my hand-some win-some John-ny.

Some say he's dark; Some say he's bonny
But the fairest of them all; Is my handsome, winsome Johnny.

I have stockings of silk; Shoes of fine green leather
Combs to bind my hair; And a ring for every finger.

Feather beds are soft; And painted rooms are bonny
But I would leave them all; To go with my love, Johnny.

I know where I'm going; And I know who's going with me
I know who I love; But the dear knows who I'll marry.

Main St. Lisdoonvarna.

The Rose of Tralee

Oh the pale moon was ris - ing a - bove the green moun - tain, the sun was de - clin - ing be - neath the blue sea, when I strayed with my love o'er the pure crys - tal foun - tain that stands in the

made me love Mar - y the Rose of Tra-

Last Time

- lee. The - lee.

The cool shades of evening their mantles were spreading
And Mary, all smiling, sat listening to me
The moon thro' the valley her pale rays was shedding
When I won the heart of the Rose of Tralee.
Tho' lovely and fair as the rose of the summer
Yet, 'twas not her beauty alone that won me,
Oh! no, 'twas the truth in her eye ever dawning
That made me love Mary, the Rose of Tralee.

Nelson St. Tralee, Co. Kerry.

Danny Boy

Andante with Expression

Oh Dan - ny Boy _____ the pipes, the pipes are

ca - ll - ing, from glen to

glen _____ and down the moun - tain

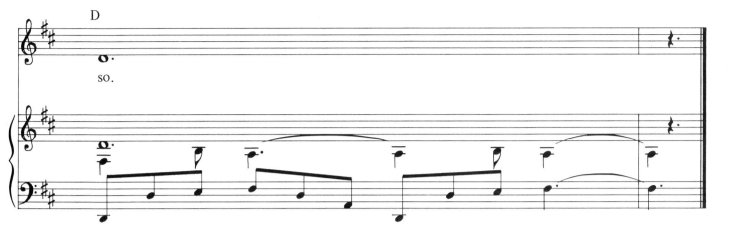

And when ye come and all the flowers are dying
If I am dead, as dead I well may be
You'll come and find the place where I am lying
And kneel and say an Ave there for me.

Repeat Chorus: —

And I shall hear tho' soft you tread above me
And all my grave will warmer sweeter be
If you will bend and tell me that you love me
Then I shall sleep in peace until you come to me.

Derry, Nth. Ireland.

Easy and Slow

would take her back home in the sweet by and

by. And what's it to an - y man whe-ther or no

whe - ther it's ea - sy or whe - ther I'm true.

As I lif - ted her pet - ti - coat ea - sy and slow and I

13

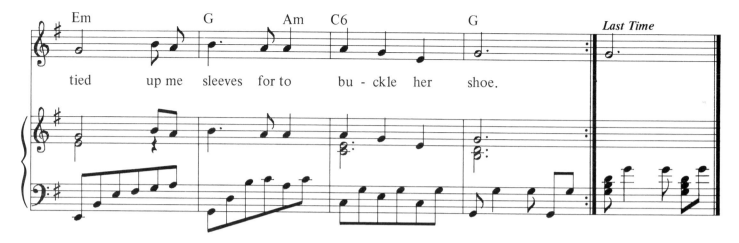

tied   up me   sleeves   for to   bu - ckle   her   shoe.

All along Thomas Street down to the Liffey
The sunshine was gone and the evening grew dark
Along by King's Bridge and begod in a jiffy
Me arms were around her beyond in the Park.

From city or country, a girl's a jewel
And well known for gripping the most of them are
But any young fella is really a fool
If he tries at the first time for to go a bit far.

And if ever you go to the town of Dungannon
You can search till your eyeballs are empty or blind
Be yeh lyin' or walkin' or sittin' or runnin'
A girl like Annie, you never will find.

The Four Courts.

14

George's St. Dungannon.

Sam Hall

Oh my name it is Sam Hall chim-ney sweep chim-ney sweep. Oh my name it is Sam Hall chim-ney sweep. _____ Oh my name it is Sam Hall _____ and I've robbed both great and small, and my neck will pay for all when I die, when I

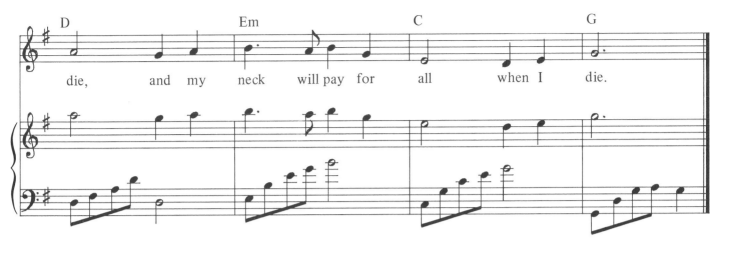

die,   and my   neck   will pay for   all   when I   die.

Oh they took me to Cootehill in a cart, in a cart
Oh they took me to Cootehill in a cart
Oh they took me to Cootehill and 'twas there I made my will
For the best of friends must part, so must I, so must I
For the best of friends must part, so must I.

Up the ladder I did grope, that's no joke, that' no joke
Up the ladder I did grope, that' no joke
Up the ladder I did grope and the hangman pulled his rope
And ne'er a word I spoke, tumbling down, tumbling down
And ne'er a word I spoke tumbling down.

(Repeat first Verse)

Turf Bog.

Paddy's Green Shamrock Shore

Our ship she lies at anchor, she's standing by the quay
May fortune bright shine down each night, as we sail over the sea
Many ships were lost, many lives it cost on the journey that lies before
With a tear in my eye I'm bidding good-bye to Paddy's Green Shamrock Shore.

So fare thee well my own true love, I'll think of you night and day
And a place in my mind you surely will find, although I am so far away
Though I'll be alone far away from my home, I'll think of the good times once more
Until the day, I can make my way back to Paddy's Green Shamrock Shore.

And now the ship is on the waves may heaven protect us all
With the wind in the sail we surely can't fail on this voyage to Baltimore
But my parents and friends did wait till the end, till I could see them no more
I then took a chance for to glance at Paddy's Green Shamrock Shore.

The Minstrel Boy

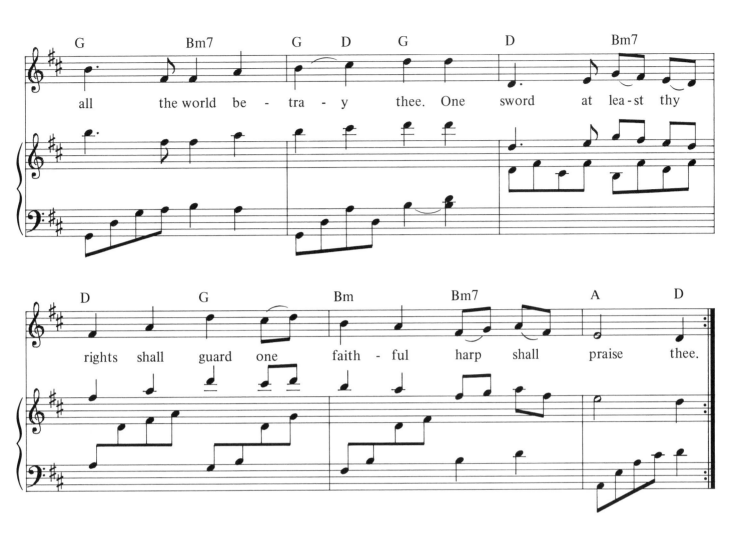

all the world be-tra-y thee. One sword at lea-st thy

rights shall guard one faith-ful harp shall praise thee.

The Minstrel fell! – but the foeman's chain
Could not bring his proud soul under
The harp he lov'd ne'er spoke again
For he tore its chords assunder
And said, "No chains shall sully thee
Thou soul of love and bravery!
Thy songs were made for the pure and free
They shall never sound in slavery"

The Snowy Breasted Pearl

Moderately Flowing

There is a Col - een fair as May for a year and for a day I have sought by ev - 'ry way her heart to gain. _____ There is no art of tongue or eye, fond youth with maid-ens try, but I've tried with cease-less si - ghs yet in vain. _____ If to France or far off

Oh! thou blooming milk-white dove, to whom I've given true love
Do not ever thus reprove my constancy
There are maidens, would be mind, with wealth in land or kine,
If my heart would but incline to turn from thee
But a kiss with welcome bland, and a touch of thy fair hand
Are all that I demand would's thou not spurn
For if not mine dear girl, oh! my snowy-breasted pearl
May I never from the fair with life return.

The Butcher Boy

In Moo-re Street where I did dwell, A but-cher boy, I loved right well. He cour-ted me my life a-way and now with me _____ he will not stay.

I wish my baby it was born
And smiling on its daddy's knee
And my poor body to be dead and gone
With the long green grass growing over me.

He went upstairs and the door he broke
And found her hanging by a rope
He took a knife and cut her down
And in her pocket these words he found.

Oh make my grave large, wide and deep
Put a marble stone at my head and feet
And in the middle a turtle dove
So the world may know I died for love.

The Cliffs Of Doneen

Take a view o'er the mountains, fine sights you'll see there
You'll see the high rocky mountains o'er the west coast of Clare
Oh the town of Kilkee and Kilrush can be seen
From the high rocky slopes round the cliffs of Doneen.

It's a nice place to be on a fine summer's day
Watching all the wild flowers that ne'er do decay
Oh the hares and lofty pheasants are plain to be seen
Making homes for their young round the cliffs of Doneen.

Fare thee well to Doneen, fare thee well for a while
And to all the kind people I'm leaving behind
To the streams and the meadows where late I have been
And the high rocky slopes round the cliffs of Doneen.

I'm A Rover

Jolly

I'm a rov - er and sel - dom so - ber, I'm a rov - er of hi - gh de-gree. For when I'm drink - ing I'm al - ways think - ing how to gain my loves com - pan - y.

Though the night be as dark as dungeon; Not a star to be seen above
I will be guided without a stumble; Into the arms of my own true love.

He stepped up to her bedroom window; Kneeling gently upon a stone
He rapped at her bedroom window; "Darling dear, do you lie alone.

It's only me your own true lover; Open the door and let me in
For I have come on a long journey; And I'm near drenched to the skin.

She opened the door with the greatest pleasure; She opened the door and she let him in
They both shook hands and embraced each other; Until the morning they lay as one.

The cocks were crawing, the birds were whistling; The streams they ran free about the brae
Remember lass I'm a ploughman laddie; And the farmer I must obey.

Now my love I must go and leave thee; And though the hills they are high above
I will climb them with greater pleasure; Since I've been in the arms of my love.

Avondale

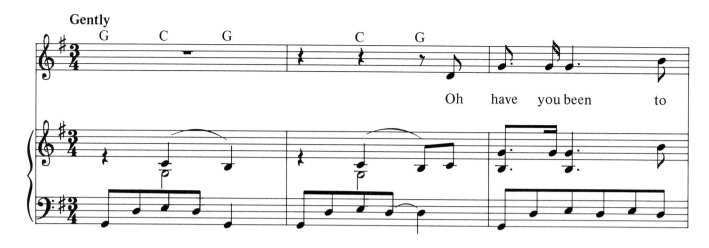

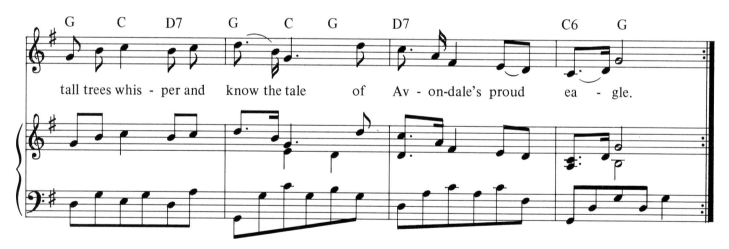

Where pride and ancient glory fade; So was the land where he was laid
Like Christ, was thirty pieces paid; For Avondale's proud eagle.

Repeat Chorus:—

Long years that green and lovely vale; Has nursed Parnell, her grandest Gael,
And curse the land that has betrayed; Fair Avondale's proud eagle.

Repeat Chorus:—

Irish Spinning Wheel.

Kelly of Killane

Andantino

What's the news what's the news O my bold Shel-ma- -lier, with your long barr-elled gu - n from the sea. _____ Say what wind from the South blows his mes - sen-ger here with a hymn of the da - wn for the free. _____ Good-ly news, good-ly news, Do I

"Tell me who is that giant with the gold curling hair
He who rides at the head of your band?
Seven feet is his height with some inches to spare
And he looks like a king in command!"
"Ah, my lads, that's the pride of the bold Shelmaliers
Among our greatest of heroes a man!
Fling your beavers aloft and give three ringing cheers
For John Kelly, the Boy from Killane

Enniscorthy's in flames, and old Wexford is won
And the Barrow to-morrow we will cross
On a hill o'er the town we have planted a gun
That will batter the gateway of Ross
All the Forth men and Bargy men march o'er the heath
With brave Harvey to lead on the van
But the foremost of all in the grim Gap of Death
Will be Kelly, the Boy from Killane

But the gold sun of freedom grew darkened at Ross
And it set by the Slaney's red waves
And poor Wexford, stript naked, hung high on a cross
And her heart pierced by traitors and slaves!
Glory O! Glory O! to her brave sons who died
For the cause of long down-trodden man!
Glory O! to Mount Leinster's own darling and pride
Dauntless Kelly, the Boy from Killane

I Know My Love

I know my love by his way of wal - king and I know my love by his way of talk - ing and I know my love dressed in his jer - sey blue and if my love leaves me what will I do an - d still she cried "I love him the

There is a dance house down in Mardyke; And there my true-love goes every night
And he takes a strange one upon his knee; And don't you think now that vexes me?

Repeat Chorus:—

If my love knew I could wash and wring; And if my love knew I could weave and spin
I'd make for him a suit of the finest kind; But the want of money leaves me behind.

James Connolly

A great crowd had gath - ered out-
- side of Kil - main - ham with their heads all un - cov - ered they knelt on the
ground. For in - side that grim pris - on lay a true Ir - ish
sold - ier. His life for his coun - try a - bout to lay down.

He went to his death like a true son of Ireland
The firing party he bravely did face
Then the order rang out: 'Present arms, Fire!'
James Connolly fell into a ready-made grave.

The black flag they hoisted, the cruel deed was over
Gone was the man who loved Ireland so well,
There was many a sad heart in Dublin that morning
When they murdered James Connolly, the Irish rebel.

Many years have rolled by since the Irish Rebellion
When the guns of Britannia they loudly did speak
And the bold I.R.A. they stood shoulder to shoulder
And the blood from their bodies flowed down Sackville Street.

The Four Courts of Dublin the English bombarded
The spirit of freedom they tried hard to quell
But above all the din came the cry: 'No Surrender!'
'Twas the voice of James Connolly, the Irish rebel.

Sackville St, now O'Connell St, Dublin.

The Waxies Dargle

Says my aul' one to your aul' one;
Will you come to the Galway Races
Says your aul' one to my aul' one;
With the price of my aul' lad's braces
I went down to Capel Street,
To the Jew man money lenders
But they wouldn't give me a couple of bob
On my oul' lad's red suspenders.

Repeat Chorus:

Says my aul' one to your aul' one;
We have no beef or mutton
But if we go to Monto Town;
We might get a drink for nuttin'
Here's a piece of advice I got
From an aul' fishmonger
When food is scarce, and you see the hearse
You'll know you have died of hunger.

Repeat Chorus:

Skibbereen

Oh fa - ther dear I of - ten hear you speak of Er - in's Isle.

Her lof - ty scenes her val - ley's green her moun - tains rude and wild. They say it

Oh, son I loved my nàtive land with energy and pride
Till a blight came o'er my crops—my sheep, my cattle died
My rent and taxes were too high, I could not them redeem
And that's the cruel reason that I left old Skibbereen.

Oh, well do I remember the bleak December day
The landlord and the sheriff came to drive us all away
They set my roof on fire with cursed English spleen
And that's another reason that I left old Skibbereen.

Your mother, too, God rest her soul, fell on the snowy ground
She fainted in her anguish, seeing the desolation round
She never rose, but passed away from life to mortal dream
And found a quiet grave, my boy, in dear old Skibbereen.

And you were only two years old and feeble was your frame
I could not leave you with my friends, you bore your father's name —
I wrapt you in my cotamore at the dead of night unseen
I heaved a sigh and bade good-bye, to dear old Skibbereen.

Oh, father dear, the day may come when in answer to the call
Each Irishman, with feeling stern, will rally one and all
I'll be the man to lead the van beneath the flag of green
When loud and high we'll raise the cry—"Remember Skibbereen".

Bunclody

Oh were I at the moss house where the birds do in - crease _____ at the foot of Mount Lein - ster or some si - lent place _____ By the streams of Bun - clo - dy that flows down so free. _____ And all that I